GRUMMAN
FIRE APPARATUS
1976-1992 PHOTO ARCHIVE

Kent D. Parrish

Iconografix
PHOTO ARCHIVE SERIES

Iconografix
PO Box 446
Hudson, Wisconsin 54016 USA

Library of Congress Control Number: 2006921105

ISBN-13: 978-1-58388-165-1
ISBN-10: 1-58388-165-4

06 07 08 09 10 11 6 5 4 3 2 1

Printed in China

Cover and book design by Dan Perry

Copyediting by Suzie Helberg

Cover photo- The Bradley-Prosperity Volunteer Fire Department in West Virginia operates this unusual solid black rig on a 1988 Ford L-9000 chassis. Serial number 18082 is equipped with a 1000-gpm pump and carries 1250 gallons of water. The department also specified a 55-foot articulating Snorkel device. The nickname of "Bingo" on the boom explains how Bradley-Prosperity was able to raise the funds to purchase the unit. This is just an example of the highly customized apparatus produced by Grumman Emergency Products in addition to meeting the basic needs of most fire departments with simple fire apparatus as well. *Kent Parrish photo*

BOOK PROPOSALS

Iconografix is a publishing company specializing in books for transportation enthusiasts. We publish in a number of different areas, including Automobiles, Auto Racing, Buses, Construction Equipment, Emergency Equipment, Farming Equipment, Railroads & Trucks. The Iconografix imprint is constantly growing and expanding into new subject areas.

Authors, editors, and knowledgeable enthusiasts in the field of transportation history are invited to contact the Editorial Department at Iconografix, Inc., PO Box 446, Hudson, WI 54016.

DEDICATION

This book is dedicated to my young son, Logan. While working on my first project, he could barely say the words "fire truck." As I started on this endeavor, he could not only enunciate those words, but can now differentiate between the types of apparatus.

FOREWORD

What began as a typical childhood fascination with fire engines has evolved into a truly enjoyable hobby and a career in the fire service. Being relatively young, I never had the pleasure (or displeasure) of riding the tailboard or fighting a non-synchronized manual transmission. Likewise, my early fire apparatus memories are not of the classics, but rather of the modern manufacturers. The Grumman wing logo is one of the first I can recall.

ACKNOWLEDGEMENTS

This book would not have been possible without the valuable assistance of fellow firefighters, buffs, and personnel within the fire apparatus industry. Their knowledge, personal records, and photographs allowed completion of this volume. Proper credit is given with each photograph. Appreciation must be extended to Bill Bruns, Dan Cimini, and Bob Pursel, formerly of Grumman Emergency Products, for taking the time to answer repetitive questions and provide technical information. I would also like to express my gratitude to the firefighters who continue to pose apparatus for dedicated photographers across the country.

It is important to note that the files of Grumman Emergency Products did not survive. There are many theories as to their fate. Regardless, every effort has been made to provide and accurately chronicle dates, model names, capacities, and serial numbers in this book. The author welcomes any additions, corrections, or clarifications.

INTRODUCTION

The name Grumman is typically associated with aeronautical innovation. It is most synonymous with aviation legends such as the World War II Wildcat and Hellcat fighter planes. However, from 1976 to 1992, the Grumman Emergency Products division was one of the largest and most well known producers of fire apparatus in America.

Decorated flight instructor and aviation designer Leroy Grumman helped start Grumman Aeronautical Engineering in 1930 by mortgaging his home. The company began by rebuilding amphibious vehicles and producing aluminum truck bodies in an abandoned auto garage in Baldwin on Long Island, New York, before receiving its first aviation contract from the United States Navy. Through innovation and efficiency, the company would go on to become one of the most important Defense contractors of the 20th Century. During peacetimes, Grumman continued its success by producing civilian aircraft such as the Agcat crop-duster and the Gulfstream executive jet. The company further established itself by designing the Lunar Landing Module, which placed the first man on the surface of the moon in 1969.

In the early 1970s, Grumman began manufacturing innovative safety products for its aerospace program. These included fire retardant suits and hoods for the astronauts and a radio controlled firefighting nozzle called the "NPO." The company saw a market for these products in the general fire service and created the Emergency Fire Service Equipment division located in Garden City, New York. With a history of building aluminum truck bodies, Grumman also introduced a complete line of ambulances and the Emergency Vehicle division was born in Montgomery, Pennsylvania.

The philosophy of Grumman Allied Industries was to apply its engineering and manufacturing skills to many commercial operations. It also set out to acquire companies with established market positions that could be enhanced by its technology. In an attempt to grow its fire and rescue business, Grumman decided to add fire apparatus to its offerings. In the early 1970s, Grumman reportedly attempted to purchase Ward LaFrance and then Young Fire Equipment. However, a deal was obviously never reached with either.

In 1976, Grumman acquired Howe Fire Apparatus of Anderson, Indiana, and its two subsidiaries, the Oren-Roanoke Corporation of Vinton, Virginia, and Coast Fire Apparatus of Martinez, California. Both Howe and Oren still had majority stockholders and the brands brought great name recognition, so Howe and Oren continued to operate separately, but were listed as subsidiaries of Grumman Allied Industries under the Emergency Vehicle division.

Grumman initially built fire apparatus in the Anderson and Vinton plants as either a Howe or Oren "by Grumman." The choice of brand depended on the customer's preference, the dealer that made the sale, or the type of apparatus that was desired. In most cases, rigs would have their respective markings and also carry the Grumman wing logo. The Martinez and Vinton plants were set up as service centers, where all brands of fire apparatus could be serviced or repaired. A handful of apparatus was also completed in Martinez.

In 1977, Grumman sent out a survey to its fire and rescue customers seeking suggestions on how to better identify the fire and rescue lines. By 1980, the two fire and rescue divisions had been consolidated into one – Grumman Emergency Products. The Martinez service center and the Anderson plant were both closed. A new state-of-the-art facility was opened in Roanoke, Virginia. Initially, standard fire apparatus were produced in Roanoke, while custom orders rolled out of the Vinton plant.

Grumman would build on the foundation laid by Howe and Oren and become a major player in the fire apparatus industry. It was soon churning out enough rigs to place it among the top four manufacturers in the United States. Grumman offered a complete line of pumping apparatus. Model names continued with the feline association of the Aeronautical division's famous World War II aircraft. The Bobcat, Minicat, and Attackcat were quick response apparatus. The pumper line consisted of the Wildcat, Firecat, and Tigercat. Model designation generally depended on the type of chassis used, the engineering involved, and pump capacity. The modular apparatus bodies were built on a steel sub-frame and available in galvanized steel or aluminum construction. Grumman would build on practically any commercial chassis that was available, with a preference towards Ford products. Custom chassis such as Hendrickson, Pemfab, and Spartan were utilized in the custom lines, with Duplex being the most prevalent. Grumman delivered apparatus all over the United States, with heavy concentrations in the Northeast, East, Southeast, and on the West Coast. International markets would include Canada, South America, the Middle East, and the Far East.

By the early 1980s, the majority stockholders of Howe and Oren began to dissipate, giving Grumman more control of the Emergency Products division. Another customer survey determined that brand preference was waning and the Grumman name had been established in the fire apparatus industry. By the end of 1983, the legendary Howe and Oren names had been phased out.

With the acquisition of Howe, Grumman became a distributor for Ladder Towers Incorporated (LTI). When this relationship ended, Grumman picked up the Hahn Fire Spire aerial ladders. Other devices included the Boardman Readi-Tower and Snorkel line. With these products, Grumman could provide an aerial apparatus to suit any customer. However, it soon began looking at establishing its own custom aerial.

Garland Kuykendall was a former LTI engineer who had started a company called Steeldraulics Products Incorporated (SPI) in Pennsylvania. Grumman knew that he had been working on his own ladder tower design and Kuykendall knew that Grumman was looking. The two soon began discussions and the 95-foot Aerialcat ladder tower was introduced in 1982. SPI built six units under a private label program before Grumman purchased the design outright. Eight more units were produced at the SPI facility before production was moved to the Vinton plant, which became known as the "Aerialcat plant." The Roanoke facility was then labeled the "pumper plant."

The Aerialcat line would expand to include 102-foot rear-mount and 92-foot mid-mount ladder towers. After seeing success with the ladder towers, Grumman began production of straight stick aerial ladders. The line would eventually include 95-, 100-, 110-, and 121-foot models.

Around 1988, the Vinton plant was closed and all operations were consolidated in Roanoke. Aerial production took place in a converted warehouse across the street from the main facility. The ladder assemblies were produced in this building and installed on the chassis across the street. Grumman had a total of three production lines, which ran according to build times. The first was the "quick line," which produced stock jobs and basic apparatus. The second built standard customs. The third produced high-end customs and finished the Aerialcats.

In 1988, Grumman began experimenting with producing its own custom cab and chassis. Initially, Grumman built the chassis for the low profile model. Truck Cab Manufacturers (TCM) constructed the cab shell and Grumman finished the interior utilizing local subcontractors. For the tilt-cab offering, Grumman fabricated the first dozen cab shells on Hendrickson Mobile Equipment (HME) chassis and had Spartan Motors finish the interiors.

It was decided that neither approach was efficient, as Grumman did not have the experience or project enough volume to fund the workforce and real estate needed for its own cab and chassis line. Duplex was then subcontracted to build the chassis for the low profile units and complete the cab interiors. After a period of time, HME replaced Duplex in supplying the chassis and finishing the cabs.

HME continued to build the chassis for the tilt-cabs, but the cab shell work was subcontracted to TCM. Spartan completed the interiors of the first 50 tilt-cabs; then HME finished the rest. The low profile offering was called the Panther I and the tilt-cab was dubbed the Panther II.

In the early 1990s, the structure within Grumman Allied Industries began to change. The corporation felt it had extended itself too far from its core Defense business. At this time, it was producing everything from yachts to buses. The Pentagon had also announced budget cutbacks, which was anticipated to affect the industry. Grumman decided to shed its commercial lines and concentrate on the Defense contracts. Attempts were made at selling the Emergency Products division and an investment group was actually lined up as a buyer. However, negotiations failed in part because of the unionized workforce.

At this time, sales were strong and turning a profit. The Emergency Products division was poised to become the industry leader. However, the Military mindset of the new streamlined corporation didn't understand the fire apparatus business and had no direction for the division. With failed attempts at selling, the decision was made to close the Emergency Products division. The announcement was made in December of 1991 and Grumman stopped taking new orders for fire apparatus. A customer was allowed to cancel an order if it was not already on the production line. However, the vast majority still wanted their Grumman and many fire departments tried unsuccessfully to place new orders. The plant was officially closed in September of 1992 after a backlog of nearly 150 fire apparatus was completed.

Many of today's fire apparatus manufacturers owe some of their success to the design and innovation of Grumman Emergency Products. Kovatch Mobile Equipment (KME) of Nesquehoning, Pennsylvania, immediately acquired the major assets of Grumman for the sole purpose of competing in the aerial market. KME also offered warranty protection on previously built Aerialcats in exchange for the design and rights to the name. To this day, the KME Aerialcat is produced at the Roanoke facility. Many former Grumman employees went to work for KME and other manufacturers. Two started M & W Fire Apparatus in Vinton after acquiring surplus equipment and bodywork. HME went on to supply its chassis and finished TCM cabs to other manufacturers and today builds complete custom fire apparatus under the revitalized Ahrens-Fox name. Northrop eventually purchased the Grumman Corporation in 1994.

Through the resources of Grumman Allied Industries, the Emergency Products division was able to introduce innovation and space-age technology to the fire apparatus industry in a span of just 16 years. Over 4,000 pieces of apparatus were produced under the Grumman name and the vast majority of these "Cats" still serve today.

When Grumman acquired Howe Fire Apparatus in 1976, it relied on the great name recognition of the legendary Howe and Oren brands to push sales. They were initially listed as subsidiaries of Grumman Allied Industries under the Emergency Products division. *Kent Parrish collection*

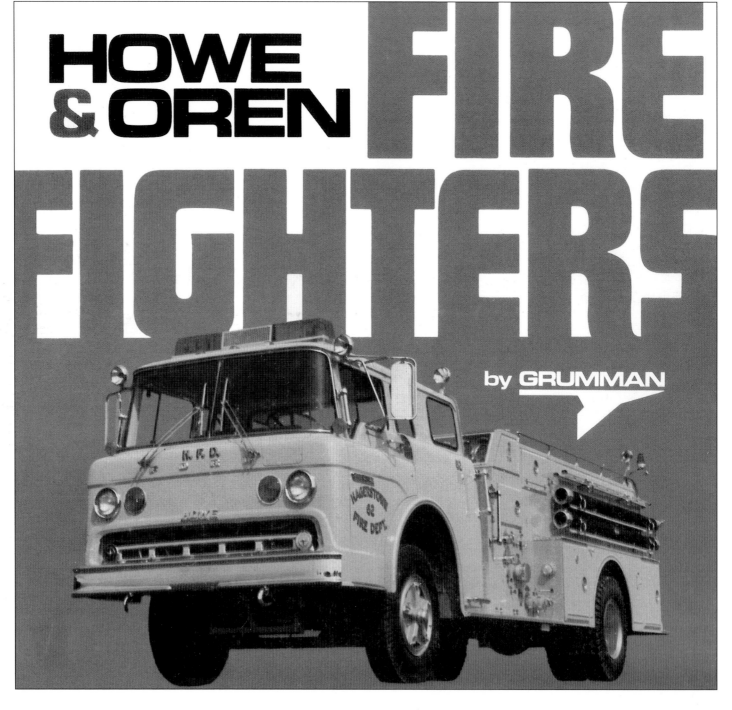

8

Grumman displayed this demonstrator model in 1976 on a Duplex R-200 chassis. Serial number 14702 was equipped with a 1250-gpm pump and 500-gallon water tank. It was eventually purchased by West Dundee, Illinois. The Howe name was prominently displayed on the front and rear of the apparatus and the Grumman wing logo appeared near the rear wheel wells. Although it is unknown who received the very first rig to feature a Grumman logo, this unit is at the very least, one of the first. *Chuck Madderom photo*

Independence, Kentucky, received two Howe-Grumman pumpers on Ford L-800 chassis in 1976. Built on short wheelbases, the units were equipped with 1000-gpm pumps and 750-gallon water tanks. They carried serial numbers 14989 and 14990. Engine 452 is pictured and still serves the department as a reserve piece. Simple apparatus such as these were common in smaller communities. *Kent Parrish photo*

This rural apparatus was purchased by New Baden, Illinois. Built on a 1976 Chevrolet C-65 chassis, the Howe-Grumman had a 750-gpm front-mount pump and 300-gallon booster tank. The front bumper extension was equipped with safety railing and short pre-connected booster lines on each side, which made for efficient work during brush fire operations. The lime rig carried serial number 15723. *Dennis J. Maag photo*

10

With the acquisition of Howe, Grumman became a distributor of LTI aerial products. This stubby quint was delivered to Coeur d'Alene, Idaho, on a 1976 Ford C-8000 chassis. Serial number 15014 was equipped with a 1000-gpm pump and 300-gallon water tank. The aerial was a three-section 65-foot rear-mount with enclosed pre-piped waterway. A cord reel provided power to the remote controlled automatic nozzle. Several units similar to this rig were produced for other departments. *Shane MacKichan photo*

It was no surprise that many of Oren's more unusual apparatus were delivered in Virginia. This Oren-Grumman was delivered to Clear Brook in Frederick County. It was built on a conventional 1977 FWD four-wheel-drive chassis. Assigned serial number 15112, the unit was equipped with a 750-gpm pump and 750-gallon water tank. The rig was originally delivered with an overhead ladder rack, which was removed and replaced by a deck gun positioned over the booster reel. *Mike Sanders photo*

The Driver Fire Department in Suffolk, Virginia, received this strange looking Oren-Grumman in 1977. It was built on the Kenworth Hustler, a cab-over-engine chassis typically found in the industrial sector. The rig was given a canopy cab extension with a rear facing bench seat. It was equipped with a 1000-gpm pump and top-mount control panel. Engine 13 carried 500 gallons of water and was assigned serial number 15110. *Jerry Puryear photo*

St. Louis, Missouri, received 22 identical Howe-Grumman pumpers on Duplex D-300 chassis in 1977. Assigned serial numbers 15238 through 15259, the lime units were equipped with 1250-gpm pumps and 500-gallon water tanks. They remained in frontline service until 1987, when St. Louis replaced its entire fleet by implementing a "Total Quint Concept." In 1990, many of the Howe-Grummans were equipped with large diameter and hard suction hose in preparation of major earthquake predictions. Three were eventually converted into Foam Units. By 2001, all but one had been traded in for a new generation of quints. The St. Louis Fire Firefighters IAFF Local 73 sequestered the remaining unit. *Dennis J. Maag photo*

This 1000-gpm Howe-Grumman pumper with 1000-gallon water tank was built on a 1977 Hendrickson 1871-S chassis and delivered to Coal City, Illinois. It was painted "Omaha Orange" and equipped with a "half top-mount" control panel, which was distinctive to Howe and Oren fire apparatus. Grumman continued the serial number sequence utilized by Howe-Oren. The majority of apparatus were simply assigned a straight number. However, some also received a suffix that designated the brand and/or which plant the apparatus was built at. For example, this apparatus carried a serial number of 15226-A. The "A" simply indicated the unit was built in Anderson. *Dennis J. Maag photo*

The Spring Lake Fire Department in Ulster, New York, took delivery of this Oren-Grumman pumper on a long nosed White conventional chassis. The long wheelbased apparatus was equipped with a 1000-gpm pump and 1000-gallon water tank. Note the hose clamp mounted on the running board behind the front fender. *Ron Bogardus photo*

The California Department of Forestry operated this Howe-Grumman in San Luis Obispo County. It was built on a 1978 Ford C-8000 chassis with two-door cab. The apparatus had a 1000-gpm main pump and 500-gallon water tank. Because of the department's primary function, the rig was also equipped with a PTO-driven 275-gpm auxiliary pump, which allowed for pump and roll operations. The unit carried a serial number of 15353-M. The "M" designated the apparatus as one of just a handful to be built in the Martinez plant under the Grumman name. *Chuck Madderom photo*

This unique apparatus was delivered to Litchfield, Connecticut. It was built on a 1978 Peterbilt conventional chassis. The rig was equipped with a 1500-gpm pump and 200-gallon water tank. The standout features were twin hose reels that each carried 2000 feet of four-inch supply hose. The unit was later converted into a traditional pumper when the reels were removed and the water tank increased. It was assigned serial number 15317-0. The "O" simply stated the rig was an Oren. *Glenn Vincent photo*

While the Oren brand held its foothold in the East, Howe was predominant in the far Northeast. Picturesque Cape Elizabeth, Maine, received this Howe-Grumman on a 1978 International Cargostar chassis with canopy cab extension. The 1000-gpm pumper had a half top-mount control panel and 500-gallon water tank. Common to Howe and Oren top-mount panels was a Plexiglas protective covering over the master gauge panel. *Frank Wegloski photo*

The West Friendship Fire Company of Howard County, Maryland, received this large Oren-Grumman pumper-tanker in 1978. Built on a Ford LST-9000 chassis, the apparatus was equipped with a 1000-gpm pump and 3000-gallon water tank. It was assigned serial number 15335. The well-stocked unit carried an abundance of portable scene lights above the compartments. A Mars 888 light, mounted on the corner of the front bumper, helped clear traffic. *Chuck Madderom photo*

Ernie Day ran New Jersey Fire Equipment, the longtime Oren dealer in that state. He had an arrangement for each Oren he sold to be called a "Great Eastern." Glassboro, New Jersey, received this 1000-gpm pumper with 750-gallon water tank on a Ford C-Series chassis. When Grumman acquired Oren through Howe, Ernie and Grumman clashed over the use of the Great Eastern name and the dealership contract was not renewed, as Grumman did not want confusion with the Oren brand. Very few Grummans were actually delivered with the Great Eastern name, which makes this rig unique. *Richard Adelman collection*

The rate of flow on the NPO, which was attached to a booster line on this rig, could be adjusted by rotating a radio transmitting cover on the nozzle. This sent a coded signal to a receiver, which was integrated into the top right-hand corner of the pump panel. Variable flow valves and engine speeds were adjusted automatically. *John Toomey photo*

The Wyandanch Fire Company on Long Island, New York, received this Oren-Grumman midi-pumper on a 1978 GMC four-wheel-drive chassis with balloon tires. The solid black unit had a 500-gpm pump and carried 500 gallons of water. The apparatus was truly unique in that it was equipped with the NPO Automated Nozzle Flow Control System, which was introduced by the Grumman Fire Service Equipment division in the early 1970s. *John Toomey photo*

This sharp looking Oren-Grumman was delivered to Green Brook, New Jersey, in 1978. Built on a Duplex R-200 chassis, it was equipped with a 1000-gpm pump and 750-gallon water tank. It was painted white over "Fruehauf Green" and carried serial number 15339. The unit was equipped with dual blue strobe beacons on the roof rather than traditional red lights. A bell was placed on the front bumper for this delivery shot, before it was permanently mounted. This rig was last seen serving Eastview-Kodak, Tennessee. *Richard Adelman collection*

This unusual Howe-Grumman was delivered to Mt. Zion, Illinois. It was built on a 1979 White Expeditor chassis with canopy cab extension and rear crew seating. The rig was equipped with a 1250-gpm pump and carried 1000 gallons of water. Grumman built several pieces of apparatus on this model of chassis, delivered primarily on the East Coast. *Bill Friedrich photo*

Arthur, Illinois, received this Howe-Grumman in 1979 built on a Chevrolet cab-over-engine chassis with extended front bumper. The 1000-gpm pumper had a half top-mount control panel and carried 1000 gallons of water. The modern light bar was added later. This apparatus was assigned serial number 15773-HV. The "HV" designated the rig as being a Howe built at the Vinton plant. *Dennis J. Maag photo*

Riverside, California, received this pumper in 1979. Powered by a Detroit Diesel 8V71N engine, it was built on a Duplex D-300 chassis. The 1500-gpm apparatus was equipped with a half top-mount control panel and big Stang gun mounted on the opposite side. Serial number 15778 carried 500 gallons of water. The Howe name was still prominently displayed on the front and both sides of the cab with the Grumman wing logo in its place near the rear wheel wells. Howe-Grumman units still carried traditional Howe characteristics, such as a hose bed rail that "broke out." *Chuck Madderom photo*

Hendrickson was a common choice of custom chassis among Grumman customers. This busy looking Oren was delivered to the Carlton Hill Fire Company of East Rutherford, New Jersey, in 1979. Painted white over lime, it was built on the 1871-S chassis. The apparatus was equipped with a 1500-gpm pump and 750-gallon water tank. The pump panel featured half top-mount controls and diamond plating all the way around. Compartment space was plentiful. *Scott Mattson photo*

In addition to the familiar square cab, Hendrickson offered a contoured cab. This big Oren-Grumman was originally delivered to Fairview, Pennsylvania, in 1979 and later acquired by Bronston, Kentucky. Serial number 15703 was mounted on the 1871-C chassis. It was equipped with a 1250-gpm pump and 1200-gallon water tank. The pump panel featured a full top-mount control panel and pre-connected "speedlay" hand lines. The white over lime rig is pictured with updated warning lights. *David Mattingly photo*

This beast was delivered to the Exxon Refinery in Benicia, California. The Howe-Grumman was built on a 1980 Duplex D-300-T chassis. Serial number 15947 was equipped with a 1000-gpm pump and carried 1000 gallons of straight foam, but no water. During this period, Grumman was a distributor of the Reading Techmatic "Readi-Tower," a competitor to Snorkel's Telesqurt. Exxon's apparatus was equipped with a 75-foot model. *Garry Kadzielawski photo*

The Union Bridge Fire Company in Carroll County, Maryland, received this Oren-Grumman on a 1980 Ford LS-9000 chassis with canopy cab extension and rear facing crew bench. The solid red apparatus featured a black gas tank and vinyl pump panel. It was equipped with a 1000-gpm pump and 1000-gallon water tank. Twin beacons were still a popular choice of warning lights at this time. Oren-Grumman units still carried traditional Oren characteristics; such as slanted beavertail compartments and hose bed rails that "broke in." *Howard Meile photo*

Company 2 of the Manhasset-Lakeville Fire Department on Long Island, New York, received this beast of a tractor-drawn aerial in 1980. The tractor was a Kenworth over-the-road model with a sleeper cab converted by Grumman into a canopy cab. The trailer was outfitted by Grumman and equipped with a 100-foot LTI aerial ladder. This rig may possibly be the only apparatus of its type to feature the Grumman name. The Kenworth tractor was eventually scrapped. The refurbished trailer and aerial ladder now serves Hilton Head Island, South Carolina, and is pulled by an American LaFrance tractor. *John Toomey photo*

Around this period, Howe-Grumman pumpers began appearing on the new Duplex D-250 chassis with square cab. Oxnard, California, received this apparatus in 1980. The yellow rig featured a 1250-gpm pump and 500-gallon water tank. It carried serial number 15999. The pre-connected crosslays, booster reel, and Stang gun were common sights at the pump area of California deliveries. Note the Grumman name is on the front of the cab, while Howe appears at the rear wheel wells. *Chuck Madderom photo*

In addition to rear-mount aerial ladders, LTI supplied Grumman with ladder tower devices as well. Waterbury, Connecticut, received this apparatus on a 1980 Duplex D-400-T chassis. It was equipped with a 100-foot ladder tower. Ground ladders were carried on the sides of the rig. The Grumman relationship would not last much longer, as LTI would soon devote its product line to Pierce Manufacturing and FMC Fire Apparatus. *Ron Bogardus photo*

Grumman introduced its Firecat line of pumpers around 1980. They were available on custom and commercial chassis with galvanized steel modular bodies on steel subframes. Pump capacity ranged from 750 to 1500 gpm. This solid black demonstrator model on a Duplex D-300 chassis was displayed at the 1980 International Association of Fire Chief's show in Kansas City, Missouri. Serial number 15898 was eventually purchased by the fire department in Marshall, Missouri. The rig was equipped with a 1250-gpm pump and carried 750 gallons of water, along with a 30-gallon foam cell. *Dennis J. Maag photo*

The commercial chassied Firecat could be built to specification or delivered quickly with limited options in a stock apparatus program. The West Atlantic City Fire Company in New Jersey received this rig on a 1980 Ford F-Series chassis. The basic unit was equipped with a 750-gpm pump and 600-gallon water tank. Air packs were mounted over the hard suction hoses. The "Firecat" logo was placed on each side of the engine hood. Scores of similar apparatus would serve small towns and rural areas across the country. *Scott Mattson photo*

After its relationship with LTI expired, Grumman began to distribute the Hahn Fire Spire aerials. This delivery to River-view, California, was one of the first such combinations. It was built on a 1981 Duplex D-400-T chassis. The tandem rear-axle apparatus was equipped with a 1250-gpm pump and 200-gallon water tank. The ladder tip configuration of the 106-foot rear-mount differed from later Fire Spire models in that it had the appearance of a Telesqurt-type device. *Chuck Madderom photo*

Pittsburgh, Pennsylvania, began taking delivery of 13 short wheelbased pumpers on Ford L-Series chassis in 1981. Although never designated as Grumman models, they were dubbed "Alleycats" because of their compact features and ability to navigate throughout the old city. The 1000-gpm rigs had varying water tank sizes, depending on the companies they were assigned to. Engine 38 carried 300 gallons. These apparatus were the first to be painted in the department's new scheme of black over yellow, in support of the city's professional baseball and football teams. *John Schmidt photo*

This delivery to the San Francisco International Airport in California may be one of the most unique pieces of apparatus ever produced under the Grumman name. The low profile Howe was constructed on an Oshkosh L-Series chassis. Despite its stealth construction, the rig was still able to accommodate a 1500-gpm pump, 500-gallon water tank, hose bed, and standard compartments. Serial number 16181 was designed in this manner to negotiate under various airport structures and inside parking garages. Although Grumman advertised a Customcat model, one was never technically designated. Specialized customs usually wound up with the Firecat name. However, this apparatus would have certainly fit the criteria. *Chuck Madderom photos*

The Rohm and Haas Chemical Company operates a well-equipped fire brigade at their plant in Louisville, Kentucky. It is located in a volatile area of town known as "Rubbertown," one of the largest concentrations of chemical plants in the nation. The facility received this 1250-gpm Firecat on a Ford C-8000 chassis with canopy cab extension in 1982. The apparatus was equipped to carry 300 gallons of water and 300 gallons of foam. It was assigned serial number 16468. *Kent Parrish photo*

Grumman introduced the Aerialcat ladder tower in 1982. The first delivery was this 95-foot model for the Friendship Fire & Hose Company of Elizabethtown, Pennsylvania. Built on a 1982 Duplex D-400-T chassis, serial number 16323 now serves Mt. Jackson, Virginia. The Aerialcat body was constructed of galvanized steel. Ground ladders could be stored internally or stacked on each side of the apparatus. The three-section steel aerial ladder had an aluminum platform that could flow up to 1500 gallons per minute with an unrestricted load of 750 pounds. Steeldraulics, a company started by a former LTI engineer, built the first six Aerialcats for Grumman. *Rick Rudisill photo*

Cincinnati, Ohio, was long known for its fleet of custom Seagrave fire apparatus. The department made a somewhat surprising move by ordering four 750-gpm pumpers on 1982 Ford C-Series commercial chassis. Grumman reportedly had to re-engineer its Firecat design to accommodate the smaller 300-gallon water tank the department preferred. The deliveries were assigned serial numbers 16549 through 16552. The apparatus took quite a pounding serving in an urban environment. They have since been refurbished and are serving various small towns in the region. *Bill Friedrich photo*

The Shelby County Fire District in Kentucky operated a large fleet of white Grumman apparatus. The department received a total of three Ford C-Series pumpers, including this C-900 with 1000-gpm pump, 600-gallon water tank, and 55-foot Readi-Tower in 1982. The unit was assigned serial number 16407. Shelby County would also later purchase a Grumman 102-foot Aerialcat and 1500-gallon tanker from Middletown in neighboring Jefferson County, Kentucky. *Kent Parrish photo*

36

Grumman delivered four identical Firecats on Duplex D-350 chassis to the largest combination paid/volunteer fire department in Kentucky. The Pleasure Ridge Park Fire District in Louisville received three consecutive units in 1982 with serial numbers 16567 through 16569. A fourth unit was delivered in 1983 with serial number 16719. The white over lime units were equipped with 1250-gpm pumps and 750-gallon water tanks. Although now out of service, these four companies fought quite a bit of fire in their lifetimes. *Greg Stapleton photo*

This Howe-Grumman pumper-tanker was delivered to Skyland, North Carolina, in 1982. The Peterbilt 320 chassis with tilt-cab was typically seen on heavy-duty industrial type vehicles, but was occasionally utilized on larger fire apparatus such as this unit. Note the exhaust stack behind the cab. Skyland's 1250-gpm rig was equipped with a full top-mount control panel and 2500-gallon water tank. Serial number 16350 was painted white with blue striping. When this apparatus was photographed, it had received updated warning lights. *Greg Stapleton photo*

Versailles, Indiana, operated two Grummans, including this rig on a 1982 Ford C-800 standard cab chassis. The Firecat was available with top-mount or side-mount control panels. Serial number 16480 was equipped with a 750-gpm pump and 1000-gallon water tank. The lime rig is lettered as "Tyson 1." The department's apparatus are named and numbered after James Tyson, a town benefactor and co-founder of the Walgreen's drugstore chain. *Kent Parrish photo*

The Grumman Wildcat was an economy apparatus built on a commercial chassis and readily available with few options. Pump capacity was limited to 1000 gpm and only side-mount control panels were available. The town of Salvo, located along the Outer Banks of North Carolina, ordered this 1000-gpm pumper with 900-gallon water tank on a 1983 Ford F-800 chassis. The department specified an overhead rack to carry a 50-foot Bangor ladder. The rig was assigned serial number 16807. *Mike Sanders photo*

The Hahn Fire Spire aerial ladders were available in 85- and 106-foot models. Kettering, Ohio, received this 106-foot quint in 1982 on a Duplex D-350-T chassis. It was equipped with a 1500-gpm pump and 250-gallon water tank. The white over yellow apparatus carried serial number 16513. The aerial was considered to be dry, as there was no pre-piped waterway. This view shows the large amount of compartment space offered when ground ladders were stored internally. *Greg Stapleton photo*

The Black Mudd Fire District in Louisville, Kentucky, received this Oren-Grumman in 1982. Built on a Duplex D-250 chassis, the 1250-gpm apparatus had a full top-mount control panel and carried 750 gallons of water. Ladders were enclosed in a special compartment underneath the rear hose bed. Serial number 16254 was painted solid white. The neighboring Okolona Fire District eventually absorbed Black Mudd, but "BMFD" was left on the front of the cab. The Oren name would soon fade away, as Grumman had determined there was no longer a strong brand preference and the majority stockholders in Howe and Oren had begun to dissipate. *Kent Parrish photo*

The Firecat would become Grumman's signature pumper. This apparatus was delivered to Galena Park, Texas, in 1982. The solid white unit was constructed on a Duplex D-300 chassis. Serial number 16399 was equipped with a 1500-gpm pump and 500-gallon water tank. The rig was photographed much later in its life, the only evidence being a modern light bar, which shows the pristine condition in which it was maintained. *Eric Hansen photo*

The Roosevelt Fire District on Long Island, New York, took delivery of this Firecat pumper on a Duplex D-300 chassis in 1983. It was equipped with a 1500-gpm pump with full top-mount control panel and speedlay attack lines. The white over lime apparatus carried 500 gallons of water. Note the turnout gear stored over the compartments, a trait common to Northeastern volunteer fire departments. *John Toomey photo*

This 95-foot Aerialcat was delivered to Palo Alto, California, in 1983. Serial number 16649 was built on a low profile Duplex D-450-T chassis and had ground ladders stored internally. After the first five Aerialcat deliveries, Grumman retained a sixth unit for testing purposes. You will note the "Force Distribution Members," which consisted of seven steel plates welded vertically to each side of the ladder base section. These were among the design improvements suggested by engineers at the same facility that performed rigorous testing for the Aerospace division. They were retrofitted to the first five deliveries and came standard on subsequent units. *Chuck Madderom photo*

Grumman utilized the Mack M-Series chassis for many apparatus. Blacksburg, Virginia, received this Firecat in 1983 on an MC686FC chassis with a canopy cab extension and rear facing bench seat. The 1500-gpm pump had full top-mount controls and the apparatus carried 500 gallons of water. Engine 3 was assigned serial number 16626. Blacksburg is a busy all-volunteer department that protects Virginia Tech University. *Kent Parrish photo*

This tandem rear-axle tanker-pumper was delivered to Fletcher, North Carolina, in 1983 on a Mack MC686FCS chassis. The two-door cab on this rig made for quite a compact apparatus. Serial number 16484 was equipped with a 300-gpm pump and a 2000-gallon water tank. Although Grumman advertised a Tankercat model, one was never actually designated. Tanker apparatus were called either Wildcats or Firecats, depending on pump capacities. *Steve Hagy photo*

The Harvey Volunteer Fire District 6 in Louisiana received this pumper on a Duplex D-350 chassis in 1983. Serial number 16658 was equipped with a big 2000-gpm pump and 500-gallon water tank. The apparatus was originally delivered in solid red. The upper cab was later painted white. The rig was equipped with a 55-foot Readi-Tower, which was now under the control of Boardman Fire Apparatus. *Greg Stapleton photo*

It only seemed natural for the Emergency Products division to provide a piece of fire apparatus for the Aerospace division. The Kennedy Space Center in Florida received this Tigercat on a Ford C-8000 chassis in 1983. Tigercats differed from Firecats in that their bodies were built entirely of aluminum, which fared much better in the salty sea air of Florida. Painted yellow, serial number 16811 was equipped with a 1250-gpm pump and 600-gallon water tank. Note the rocket in the background of the photograph. Because of such hazards, the apparatus also carried 100 gallons of foam and 200 pounds of dry chemical powder. *Garry Kadzielawski photo*

Hartford, Connecticut, received this 106-foot rear-mount on a Duplex D-350 chassis in 1983. The single rear-axle configuration made for quite a compact truck company in the congested inner city streets. This rig was assigned serial number 16614. Four A-style outriggers stabilized the apparatus. Grumman built approximately eight units with the Hahn Fire Spire aerial. *Mike Bakunis photo*

Sullivan, Illinois, was a loyal Howe customer and continued to do business with Grumman. The department's fleet was painted a striking royal blue color. This pumper was completed in 1983 on a Duplex D-350 chassis. It was equipped with a 1000-gpm pump and half top-mount panel. A 300-gpm PTO-driven auxiliary pump enabled the unit to mount pump and roll operations. The apparatus carried 1000 gallons of water and 10 gallons of foam. Carrying serial number 16609, this apparatus was one of the last to feature the Howe name. *Dennis J. Maag photo*

The Public Service Electric & Gas Company of New Jersey protected its Salem and Hope Creek nuclear generating stations in Hancock's Bridge with this impressive Firecat. Engine 1 was built on a 1983 Ford C-8000 chassis and equipped with a 1250-gpm pump. It carried 750 gallons of water and 140 gallons of AFFF. A large turret was mounted on the cab roof and an overhead rack carried ground ladders and a Stokes basket. The elongated pump panel was necessary to house the foam system. The rig was painted in a unique white, yellow, and orange scheme. *Howard Meile photo*

Grumman delivered many apparatus to big-city urban fire departments. A group of Firecats on Hendrickson 1871-W chassis was delivered to Detroit, Michigan, in 1982. They carried serial numbers 16419 through 16423. The apparatus were equipped with 1250-gpm pumps, 600-gallon water tanks, and 25-gallon foam cells. *Steve Hagy photo*

San Francisco, California, received two Firecats on Duplex D-350 chassis in 1983. They carried serial numbers 16543 and 16544. Each was equipped with a 1500-gpm pump and 600-gallon water tank. Note the lack of warning lights on the front face of the cab. Flashing lights were mounted on the cab roof on either side of the warning beacon. *Chuck Madderom photo*

This 95-foot unit was delivered to Holland Charter Township, Michigan, in 1984. While the majority of Aerialcats were built on Duplex chassis, this apparatus was constructed on a Spartan Monarch. Serial number 16771 was equipped with a 1500-gpm pump and 200-gallon water tank. Four H-style outriggers with 18-foot spreads provided stabilization. Although Grumman purchased the Aerialcat design after production of the first six units, eight more would be fabricated at the Steeldraulics facility before production was moved to the Vinton plant. *Chuck Madderom photo*

Grumman built several pieces of apparatus utilized as airport crash rigs. Addison, Texas, received this Attackcat in 1984 on a Chevy C-65 four-wheel-drive chassis. Assigned serial number 16798, the solid white rig was equipped with a 300-gpm pump and 500-gallon water tank. It also carried 60 gallons of foam and 400 pounds of dry chemical powder, which could be applied through a roof mounted turret or a specialized booster reel. The Grumman Attackcat midi-pumpers were quick response apparatus built on medium-duty commercial chassis with aluminum modular bodies and pumps up to 1000 gpm. *Steve Hagy photo*

Louisville, Kentucky, operated two Grumman foam-pumpers as part of its Hazardous Materials Team. Engine 5 was built on a 1984 Duplex D-260 chassis. It was equipped with a 1000-gpm pump and assigned serial number 17105. The rig carried 700 gallons of water and 300 gallons of foam. The compartment format with combination ladder on the driver's side was typical to Louisville specifications. Engine 1 operated a similar model on a 1982 Duplex D-350 chassis. *Greg Stapleton photo*

Buffalo, New York, received this Firecat on a 1984 Duplex D-350 chassis. It was equipped with a 1250-gpm pump and 600-gallon water tank. Of special note is the way the ground ladders were stored. They simply slid into a slot behind the compartment doors on the officer's side of the apparatus. *Bill Friedrich photo*

Grumman soon added a 102-foot model with an unrestricted 800-pound tip load rating to the Aerialcat line. Aluminum body construction and dual platform monitors were added to the option list as well. The Laurelton Fire Company of Brick Township, New Jersey, received this unit in 1984. Serial number 16974 was built on a Duplex D-350-T chassis and featured a 1500-gpm pump with 200-gallon water tank. An uncommon request on apparatus of this type was the addition of a booster reel. *Scott Mattson photo*

The Grumman Minicat featured an aluminum modular body mounted on a one-ton pickup-style chassis and pump capacity of up to 500 gpm. Some larger cities operated such vehicles for quick response and rescue capabilities, although they were more common in small town departments. Richmond, Virginia, received this neat little unit on a 1984 GMC 3500 four-wheel-drive chassis. It was equipped with a 400-gpm pump and 250-gallon water tank. Warning lights were mounted for clearance under low profile areas. The apparatus was assigned serial number 16917. *Bill Friedrich photo*

The Grumman Bobcat was designed primarily as a brush unit. Also mounted on a one-ton pickup-style chassis, it featured an aluminum body with a skid-mounted firefighting unit consisting of a 160-gpm gasoline powered pump and 250-gallon water tank. The seaside town of Longport, New Jersey, received this unit on a 1984 GMC 3500 four-wheel-drive chassis. The department converted it to a rescue unit by later removing the pump and tank. Ladders and even a surfboard were carried on an overhead rack. *Jack Wright photo*

This 102-foot Aerialcat was delivered to Atlantic Highlands, New Jersey. It was built on a 1984 Spartan low profile chassis and painted white over yellow. Serial number 16904 was equipped with a 1500-gpm pump and 200-gallon water tank. The Aerialcats featured the only true modular aerial body in the industry at this time. Grumman extended a 10-year structural warranty on the aerial, torque box, and outriggers. The structural design exceeded ANSI standards with a 3 to 1 safety factor. *John Rieth photo*

Industry wide, Spartan was a popular choice of custom chassis. The historic United Fire Company of Fredrick, Maryland, received this Firecat on a 1984 Gladiator chassis with fully enclosed Command Cab. The apparatus was equipped with a 1250-gpm pump and 1000-gallon water tank. A chrome trim band wrapped around the mid-section of the cab. *Howard Meile photo*

The city of Lansing, Michigan, took delivery of two Firecats on Spartan Monarch chassis in 1984. They were assigned serial numbers 17242 and 17243. Each was equipped with a 1250-gpm pump and 600-gallon water tank. The pumpers complimented a Grumman Aerialcat already on the roster. Lansing's fleet was traditionally painted mostly white with red lower compartments. *Steve Hagy photo*

Inglewood, California, received this 102-foot Aerialcat in 1985. While the cab may appear to be a Duplex D-450, it was actually the Hendrickson version. Serial number 17219 did not have a pump and tank. Ground ladders were stored internally. Every Grumman Aerialcat was subjected to rigorous testing before delivery. A unique proof load test for trussed ladders consisted of anchoring the chassis to the ground and running the aerial straight off the back of the apparatus. Each ladder section was stressed with various weights, which was accomplished by filling special containers with water. Subsequent testing was also recommended throughout the lifetime of each unit. *Chuck Madderom photo*

Several Grumman pumpers took some long delivery trips. This Firecat pumper was sent to Juneau, Alaska, in 1985. Here, the Glacier Volunteer Fire Department placed the apparatus into service. Built on a Hendrickson 1871-WS chassis, it was one of several similar rigs delivered to Alaskan fire departments. The 1500-gpm units were equipped with top-mount control panels and 1000-gallon water tanks. Ladders were stored on officer side racks. Grumman also sent pumpers on Mack MS chassis to Bermuda. *Bill Friedrich photo*

This 102-foot Aerialcat was originally yellow and delivered to Ventura, California, in 1985. After a short period of service, it was sold to the Camp Taylor Fire District in Louisville, Kentucky, where it was repainted white over red and still serves to this day. It was built on a Duplex D-450-T chassis. Serial number 17426 was equipped with a 1500-gpm pump and 200-gallon water tank. Camp Taylor carries a special rescue chute that attaches to the platform. In a rescue situation, occupants enter the elevated platform and zip to safety via the rescue chute. *Kent Parrish photo*

The Elk Grove Fire District in California received this unique Firecat pumper. It was built on a GMC TopKick chassis and powered by a Caterpillar 3208 diesel engine. The rig was equipped with a 1000-gpm Waterous pump mounted on a massive front bumper extension. The body carried a 750-gallon water tank. The apparatus was assigned serial number 17219. Elk Grove operated several Grumman apparatus over the years. *Chuck Madderom photo*

In a few instances, Grumman completed apparatus on another manufacturer's custom chassis. This delivery was one of at least two Grummans built on Hahn custom chassis. The Albion Fire Company in Winslow Township, New Jersey, received this apparatus in 1985. It was equipped with a 2000-gpm pump and carried 650 gallons of water with a 30-gallon foam cell. After Boardman Fire Apparatus ended their relationship, Grumman became a distributor of the Snorkel products. This rig had a 50-foot Telesqurt. *Scott Mattson photo*

Broadview, Illinois, received this 102-foot Aerialcat on a low profile 1985 American LaFrance Century-Series chassis. It was equipped with a 2000-gpm pump and 300-gallon water tank. The rig was assigned Grumman serial number 17110. Note the pre-piped deck gun atop the pump area. The engineering and cost associated with producing an Aerialcat on such an unfamiliar chassis resulted in Grumman rejecting subsequent requests. *Garry Kadzielawski photo*

This big Firecat pumper-tanker was delivered to Western Wake, North Carolina. It was built on a 1985 Kenworth L-700 chassis. This is another chassis typically seen on heavy-duty industrial vehicles, but occasionally used in the fire service. In this case, a canopy cab and rear facing bench seating was added. A safety gate was later added along with updated warning lights. The apparatus was equipped with a 1000-gpm pump and full top-mount control panel. Serial number 17232 carried 2500 gallons of water. *Greg Stapleton photo*

Fire Company No. 2 in Pennsauken, New Jersey, operated this very unusual aerial apparatus. Grumman built the unit on a low profile 1985 Pemfab Sovereign chassis. The rig was equipped with a 103-foot articulating Simon Snorkel, a device typically seen in the European fire service. It was similar to the American Snorkel, but was equipped with a rescue ladder that was attached to the sides of each section and a standing platform at the bend of the device. Pennsauken's unit was equipped with an abundance of ground ladders and scene lights. *Scott Mattson photo*

The Reliance Fire Company of Woodstown, New Jersey, operates a sharp looking fleet of lime apparatus with green strip-ing. This 1986 Grumman Tigercat was no exception. It was built on a 1986 Pemfab Imperial chassis. The 1000-gpm rig was equipped with top-mount controls and speedlay attack lines. Black vinyl covered the top and side pump panels. Twin booster reels, a deck gun, and a 1000-gallon water tank rounded out its features. A chrome trim band wrapped around the lower portion of the cab. *Scott Mattson photo*

This 102-foot Aerialcat was originally delivered to Westerville, Ohio, and painted lime. It is pictured at its new home of Mt. Horeb, Wisconsin, a favorite among many fire apparatus buffs. This department operates a striking fleet of solid black apparatus with red striping, ornate lettering, and an abundance of gold leafing. The rigs are equipped with every bell and whistle imaginable. Truck 1 was mounted on a 1986 Duplex D-350-T chassis with fully enclosed cab. Dual bells and Mars 888 lights were mounted on the front bumper and old school warning beacons, common to Mt. Horeb apparatus, were added. Serial number 17689 is equipped with a 1250-gpm pump and 300-gallon water tank. *Garry Kadzielawski photo*

The Amador Fire Protection District in Jackson, California, acquired this tandem rear-axle unit from Guerneville, California. It was built on a 1986 Ford C-Series chassis with canopy cab extension. Truck 1 was equipped with a 1250-gpm pump and 500-gallon water tank. Serial number 17562 carried a 75-foot Telesqurt device. Note the gasoline powered portable generator located above the pump panel area behind the crosslays. This inexpensive option would eventually give way to diesel and hydraulically powered units. *Garry Kadzielawski photo*

When Mack ceased production of complete fire apparatus in 1984, it still made the popular CF chassis available for other manufacturers to complete the bodywork on, which Grumman did on numerous units. Shelbyville, Kentucky, received this Firecat on a 1986 CF686FC chassis. It was equipped with a 1250-gpm pump and 600-gallon water tank. The unit had standard equipment of the day – two crosslays, a booster reel, and pre-piped deck gun. To a fire apparatus purist and Mack fan, this was a sharp looking and uncluttered rig. It was solid red with chrome wheels, had minimal warning equipment, and simple markings. *Greg Stapleton photo*

This Tigercat airport crash rig was delivered to Hammond, Louisiana. It was built on a Ford C-900 four-wheel-drive chassis. The 1250-gpm apparatus carried 1000 gallons of water and 50 gallons of foam, which could be applied through a roof mounted turret or a specialized booster reel. Combination rigs such as these proved more efficient for smaller departments as opposed to an airport staffing a full-fledged crash rig. Serial number 17539 complimented a standard Ford C-900 pumper delivered in the same year. *Steve Hagy photo*

The Carova Beach Volunteer Fire Department is responsible for protecting a remote area along the Outer Banks of North Carolina. The seashore is actually the main route into and out of the community. In order to navigate this sandy terrain, the department had Grumman build this Tigercat pumper on a four-wheel-drive International S-1800 chassis with front balloon tires. The 1000-gpm unit had top-mount controls and carried 1000 gallons of water. Serial number 17498 was painted solid white. *Mike Sanders photo*

The North Tahoe Fire Protection District in California is responsible for protecting a very diverse terrain and must also be prepared to operate during adverse weather conditions. Grumman delivered this Firecat on a Duplex D-450 four-wheel-drive chassis in 1987. The solid white apparatus was equipped with a 1500-gpm pump and 750-gallon water tank. A hard cover protected the hose bed from flying wildfire embers and Mother Nature. The apparatus was assigned serial number 17581. *Chuck Madderom photo*

The Middletown Fire Protection District in Louisville, Kentucky, received two of these tankers on 1987 Ford C-8000 chassis. The rigs were purchased primarily for interstate response. They were equipped with 475-gpm pumps, deck guns, crosslays, and rear hose beds. The units carried 1500 gallons of water and 40-gallon foam cells. An additional 20 five-gallon buckets of foam were stored in the hose bed. Originally delivered solid red, the upper cabs were later painted black. The apparatus were assigned serial numbers 17858 and 17859. Both were eventually sold to departments in neighboring counties. *Greg Stapleton photo*

Washington D.C. received two 102-foot Aerialcats without pumps and tanks in the department's patriot white, red, and stars scheme. Serial numbers 17774 and 17775 were built on 1987 Duplex D-450-T chassis. The forward most compartments were cut short with the addition of recessed crew seating, a specification common to the department's truck companies. Ground ladders were stored internally. An Aerialcat also served neighboring Arlington County, Virginia. *Richard Adelman photo*

The Mystic Island Fire Company is one of three volunteer fire companies protecting Little Egg Harbor Township in Ocean County, New Jersey. This big tandem rear-axle Firecat was delivered in 1987. It was built on the new Duplex D-500 Vanguard tilt-cab chassis, which featured a full-length rear-facing bench seat. The apparatus was equipped with a 1500-gpm pump, 3000-gallon water tank, and 100-gallon foam cell. The Grumman lineup had been streamlined. The quick response line still included the Minicat and Attackcat, but all pumpers and tankers were now designated Firecats, no matter the pump capacity or type of body construction. The Wildcat and Tigercat names were discontinued. *Scott Mattson photo*

The Lisbon Volunteer Fire Company 4 of Howard County, Maryland, operates a fleet of all-wheel-drive pumpers. This monster was delivered in 1987 on a Ford F-800 four-wheel-drive chassis with four-door cab. The extended front bumper contained a 1250-gpm pump and corner marker poles. The body featured standard compartments and carried a 600-gallon water tank. The rear wheel fender panel was diamond plated. *Richard Adelman photo*

This beast was delivered to the Department of Airports in Sacramento County, California. It was built on a 1988 Duplex D-350-T six-wheel-drive chassis. Painted "FAA" yellow, the apparatus was equipped with a 1250-gpm pump and 1500-gallon water tank. It also carried 200 gallons of AFFF and 200 pounds of halon, which could be applied via remote controlled roof and bumper turrets. Serial number 17837 had a 55-foot articulating Snorkel, which was able to maneuver up and over aircraft or the various airport structures during an emergency. *Chuck Madderom photo*

Grumman introduced its own chassis and low profile cab for the Aerialcats in 1988. Initially, Grumman fabricated the chassis and subcontracted the cab shell work to TCM. Grumman finished the cab interiors utilizing local subcontractors. Christiansburg, Virginia, received this 102-foot Aerialcat on the new 94-inch-wide Panther I chassis in 1988. Serial number 18031 was equipped with a 1500-gpm pump and 200-gallon water tank. *Kent Parrish photo*

The new low profile Panther I chassis was also available for the pumper line. The Boring Volunteer Fire Company in Maryland received this unit in 1988. Engine 422 was equipped with a 1500-gpm pump and 1000-gallon water tank. The yellow rig had a white cab roof with the "The Panther" nickname and logo. The half-doors between the cab and pump panel would be a popular option on the early Panther I models. With the chassis so low to the ground, it offered firefighters sitting in the jump seats an added measure of safety from the roadway. *Frank Wegloski photo*

Grumman also introduced the 96-inch-wide Panther II in 1988. The fully enclosed tilt-cab was in compliance with new NFPA standards that had yet to be released. Cabs were available in three different configurations. Grumman initially built the first dozen cab shells itself on HME chassis and had Spartan finish the interiors. The Grumman-built cab could be identified from the later TCM cabs in that it had a brow around the top of the cab, vertical side air vents, and a square front grille. Slovan, Pennsylvania, received this unit with 1250-gpm pump and 750-gallon water tank. *John Schmidt photo*

The Independent Hose Company of Frederick claims to be the oldest volunteer fire company in the state of Maryland. This 102-foot Aerialcat served as a demonstrator model, which the fire company purchased and repainted green over white. Serial number 18039 was built on a 1988 Panther I chassis. It was equipped with a 1500-gpm pump and 200-gallon water tank. Sadly, the apparatus later caught fire while being serviced at the Vinton plant and was declared a total loss. The fire company replaced it with a brand new Emergency-One ladder tower. *Mike Sanders photo*

The city of Mt. Pleasant, Tennessee, provided its department with this apparatus and a new fire station to help protect a growing portion of its service area and a small airport. The unit was designed as a combination structural/crash rig. Engine 3 was built on a 1988 Duplex D-350 chassis. Structural firefighting was accomplished with a 1250-gpm pump and 1000-gallon water tank. For aircraft emergencies, the rig carried 60 gallons of AFFF and was equipped with an Ansul 200-pound Purple K system. These agents could be applied via a roof-mounted turret or a special booster reel mounted behind the engine doghouse. The solid white apparatus was assigned serial number 17977. *Kent Parrish photo*

The Grumman 92-foot mid-mount Aerialcat was designed to compete with other manufacturers who offered similar devices. It was a true ladder tower, while the others were of box construction. The model was based on the heavy-duty Spartan Gladiator chassis. It was available with or without pump and tank. Unique to the Grumman quint configuration was a rear-mount pump and control panel, which removed noise and congestion away from the mid-mount turn table. Morristown, Tennessee, received this rig in 1988. Serial number 17557 was equipped with a 1500-gpm pump and 400-gallon water tank. *Greg Stapleton photo*

Grumman introduced its first straight stick Aerialcat in 1988. An outside engineer designed the 110-foot model. It had a four-section steel aerial with 500-pound tip load rating. Because the unit was very labor intensive and expensive to build, it was not deemed a promising product. The only unit built was assigned serial number 17487. It was placed on a Duplex D-350-T chassis and featured a 1500-gpm pump with 300-gallon water tank. The Macon Fire Department in Bibb County, Georgia, purchased the apparatus. *David Organ photo*

This apparatus from the East Dover Fire Company in Dover Township, New Jersey, is proof that big things can come in small packages. Grumman delivered this mini "Super Pumper" on a 1989 Ford F-350 four-wheel-drive chassis. The unit augmented the department's large diameter hose tender. Together, these two apparatus supported an inefficient hydrant system. The driving force of the Super Pumper was a skid-mounted Hale 2750-gpm single-stage pump with Chrysler 440-cubic-inch industrial engine that was recycled from an older unit and overhauled by department members. A six-inch discharge was equipped with a manifold gated down to four 2-1/2-inch outlets. The unit was assigned serial number 18181. *Scott Mattson photos*

After the failure of the 110-foot straight stick, Grumman decided to simply remove the bucket and support arms from their successful Aerialcat ladder tower design. The result was a 95-foot model. It retained the same tip load rating the ladder tower had. Without the bucket and support arms, the ladder actually had a much higher capability, but a higher rating was impractical. At least three 95-foot units were produced. Franklin, Virginia, received this rig in 1989 on a Panther I chassis. Serial number 18215 had a 1500-gpm pump and 300-gallon water tank. *Jerry Puryear photo*

International Harvester had introduced a new commercial cab and chassis, which became widely accepted by the fire service. Palmyra, Indiana, took delivery of this Firecat on the 4900 chassis in 1989. Serial number 18202 was equipped with a 1000-gpm pump and 1000-gallon water tank. While they may not catch the eye of an enthusiast, apparatus such as these were the backbone of small town fire departments across the country. *Kent Parrish photo*

With little success thus far in the ladder market, Grumman decided to offer the tallest steel ladder in the United States. Inserting the fourth section of the original 110-foot design into the three-section 100-foot model produced the 121-foot model. It had a tip load rating of 250 pounds while flowing water and 500 pounds dry. Newport, Kentucky, received this unit in 1989. Built on the Panther I chassis, it was equipped with a 1250-gpm pump and 250-gallon water tank. Truck 912 carried serial number 18126. Approximately eight of these models were built, with four going to Cleveland, Ohio. *Greg Stapleton photo*

This Firecat pumper was delivered to the Taunton Fire Company in Medford Township, New Jersey. It was built on a 1989 Simon-Duplex D-500 Vanguard chassis. Simon was a European company that had purchased the former Duplex Truck Division of the Nolan Company. Engine 2524 was equipped with a 1500-gpm pump and carried 1000 gallons of water. Pull-out stands were installed underneath the operator's stands and on both sides of the rear wheels. These allowed for extra standing area to access the crosslays and the lengths of hard suctions mounted on the upper body. *Scott Mattson photo*

The Shaker Road Fire Department in Loudonville, New York, received this 102-foot Aerialcat in 1989 without pump and tank. It was assigned serial number 18171. The department chose a Spartan Gladiator chassis because the spacious cab allowed for more head and leg room than the Panther I. However, the apparatus was quite a bit taller as a result. Just a couple of Aerialcats were built on Spartan chassis of this vintage. *Bill Friedrich photo*

Clark County, Nevada, received this Panther II pumper in 1989. After the trial period of building the cab shells itself, Grumman contracted the work to TCM and had Spartan finish the interiors of the first 50 cabs. This "compact four-door" model measured 40 inches from the center of the front wheel to the rear cab wall. Its six-person cab featured two rear-facing crew doors that opened up into a walkway between the pump housing. Painted chrome yellow, serial number 18166 was equipped with a 1250-gpm pump and 500-gallon water tank. *Chuck Madderom photo*

The innovative Grumman "Triple Threat" Firecat was like nothing offered before. The unique rear-mount design gave the pump operator 270 degrees of fire scene visibility. Two speedlay attack lines were located near the control panel and discharges were located across the rear. The Foot Hills Fire District in California received two units on 1989 Simon-Duplex D-500 Vanguard chassis. They were assigned serial numbers 18195 and 18196. The 1750-gpm pumpers carried 500 gallons of water. Booster reels were tucked away in lower compartments and a remote controlled deluge gun was mounted midship. Soon after these rigs were delivered, the fire district adopted the name of Rancho Cucamonga. *Chuck Madderom photos*

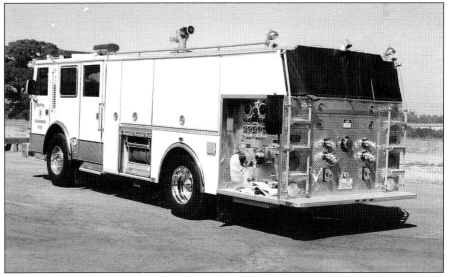

Aberdeen, Maryland, received this 102-foot Aerialcat in 1989. Serial number 18208 was equipped with a 1500-gpm pump and 160-gallon water tank. Note the uncharacteristic compartment configuration. After Grumman's trial period of producing the low profile chassis itself, Simon-Duplex was contracted to supply the chassis for the Aerialcats and finish the cab interiors. Aerialcats featured "feather-touch" controls, which ensured jolt-free movement of the aerial during operations. Options included full extension and electrical proximity alarms. *Howard Meile photo*

This Firecat was delivered to the Harrods Creek Fire District in Louisville, Kentucky. It was built on a "short-door" Duplex D-500 Vanguard chassis. Serial number 18315 was equipped with a 1500-gpm pump and 600-gallon water tank. Ground ladders were carried on both sides of the apparatus, nearly qualifying the rig as a quad. Harrods Creek also operated a Grumman 50-foot Telesqurt on a 1984 Hendrickson chassis. *Kent Parrish photo*

Comparatively, Grumman delivered very few apparatus to the Pacific Northwest. However, three of these Firecats were delivered to Tacoma, Washington, in 1989. The white over yellow rigs were assigned serial numbers 18067 through 19069. Each was built on a Spartan Gladiator chassis with rear facing crew doors leading out to a top-mount pump panel. The 1500-gpm units carried 500 gallons of water and 100 gallons of foam. One of the rigs was damaged in an accident while being delivered. The department purchased the unit from the insurance company, repaired it in-house, and eventually placed it in service. Tacoma received a fourth unit in 1990. *Shane MacKichan photo*

Inver Grove Heights, Minnesota, received this 102-foot Aerialcat in 1989 on a Simon-Duplex D-450-T chassis. Serial number 17948 was equipped with a 1500-gpm pump and 200-gallon water tank. A few late-model Aerialcats had the Simon-Duplex cab rather than the Grumman Panther I. While similar in design and both built by TCM, the Simon-Duplex and Panther I cabs did have visual differences. You will note that the head and warning light bezels on the Simon-Duplex cabs angle to an outer point. The side windows are rectangular. The raised roof portion of the cab was only slight and all four doors were the same height. *Paul Barrett photo*

Located along the Outer Banks of North Carolina, the town of Carolla received this 102-foot Aerialcat in 1990 on a Panther I chassis. Serial number 18292 was painted white with a blue band. It was equipped with a 1500-gpm pump and 250-gallon water tank. You will note that the head and warning light bezels on the Panther I cab were squared off. The side windows are narrower and come down to the mid-line of the cab. The crew doors fit into the raised roof cab, which was taller and typically featured front facing port windows. *Mike Sanders photo*

Mount Laurel, New Jersey, received this Panther II pumper in 1990. Engine 3632 was equipped with a 1500-gpm pump and 1000-gallon water tank. The "long four-door" cab measured 67-1/2 inches from the center of the front wheel to the rear cab wall and was capable of seating six to ten personnel. HME would replace Spartan in finishing the TCM cabs. The body featured lower rear compartments that extended all the way to the rear and the addition of side facing light bars was becoming a trend. Mount Laurel also operated a 1988 102-foot Aerialcat. *Scott Mattson photo*

This 1990 Panther I pumper was delivered just down the road to the busy Roanoke County Fire & Rescue station in Hollins, Virginia. Engine 5 was equipped with a 1250-gpm pump and 750-gallon water tank. Serial number 18469 was painted in the department's two-tone scheme of white and lime. The unit carried several buckets of foam above the driver's side compartments. Roanoke County had received earlier Grumman pumpers on Duplex, Ford, and Kenworth chassis. *Kent Parrish photo*

Grumman delivered at least six Aerialcats to Canadian fire departments. This 102-foot model went to Burlington, Ontario. It was constructed on a 1990 Pemfab Imperial chassis, a popular choice in Canada. The apparatus was equipped with a 1250-gpm pump. Serial number 18270 carried 120 gallons of water and 40 gallons of foam. The rig was actually intended to run an engine company, but its small tank and cumbersome size proved to be inefficient. *Dave Stewardson photo*

HME also provided a heavy-duty conventional chassis, which was primarily utilized in the construction industry. However, a handful of the VT-100 chassis were utilized for fire apparatus. Alpine Township, Michigan, received this Firecat with 1250-gpm pump and 750-gallon water tank on the VT-100 in 1990. Assigned serial number 18403, the apparatus was painted in a sharp white and red scheme. *Garry Kadzielawski photo*

The Mission Fire Company of Bordentown Township, New Jersey, received this versatile apparatus in 1990. The white over yellow rig was built on the Simon-Duplex D-500 Vanguard chassis. Squrt 3212 featured a big 1750-gpm pump and carried 500 gallons of water. The Snorkel products continued to be popular additions. This rig was equipped with a 65-foot Telesqurt. *Scott Mattson photo*

Historic Charlestown, Maryland, was chartered in 1742. The town layout is virtually unchanged with its original core of 12 streets. To navigate the street grid, the town's volunteer fire company received this short wheelbased Panther II pumper in 1990. The six-person "standard four-door" cab measured 48 inches from the center of the front wheel to the rear cab wall. The 1250-gpm apparatus was equipped with a black vinyl control panel and 1000-gallon water tank. *Howard Meile photo*

Atlanta, Georgia, received four 92-foot mid-mount Aerialcats without pumps and tanks on Spartan Gladiator chassis. The first three were assigned serial numbers 18055 through 18057 and delivered in 1988. One of these was soon sold to Taftville, Connecticut. Serial number 18383 was painted "FAA" yellow and assigned as Y-7 at Hartsfield International Airport in 1990. The original Grumman mid-mount design had two features that were soon modified. One was a set of access ladders that hung down from the platform. These created maneuverability problems and were deleted from the design. Also, four H-style outriggers stabilized the original unit. A single down-rigger was added to the front facing of the cab to increase the working height of the unit. *David Organ photo*

The Thorofare Fire Company of West Deptford Township, New Jersey, received this Triple Threat Firecat in 1990 on a short-door Simon-Duplex D-500 Vanguard chassis. The apparatus was painted a striking teal color with white cab roof. A hydraulic motor connected to a crankshaft PTO-operated hydraulic pump drove the 1750-gpm rear-mount pump. Because the hydraulic system acted as a variable transmission, the truck engine was allowed to operate at very efficient levels. This compact unit carried 500 gallons of water. *Jack Wright photo*

The Vails Gate Fire District in upstate New York received one of the five original 95-foot Aerialcat deliveries in 1982. After just eight years of service, the department replaced it with this 102-foot model in 1990. The new Truck 482 featured a Panther I cab on a Simon-Duplex chassis. It was equipped with a 1500-gpm pump and 300-gallon water tank. Serial number 18284 was painted white over lime. *John M. Calderone photo*

The Lyndon Fire Protection District in Louisville, Kentucky, received this Firecat in 1990 on a Mack CF690FC chassis. Late model Mack CF chassis came stock with only an extended cab roof. Grumman added the rear walls, seats, windows, and doors to finish the cab. The apparatus was equipped with a 1500-gpm pump and 500-gallon water tank. Engine 1634 was assigned serial number 18316. *Kent Parrish photo*

Four Firecats were delivered to Chesterfield, Virginia, on 1991 Mack CF688FC chassis. Painted white over yellow, the apparatus carried serial numbers 18601 through 18604. The units were equipped with 1000-gpm pumps and 500-gallon water tanks. Mack would cease production of the venerable CF chassis in the following year. *David Mattingly photo*

This sharp looking Panther II pumper-tanker was delivered to the Malaga Fire Company of Franklin Township, New Jersey, in 1991. The apparatus featured a long four-door cab with raised roof. It was painted white over lime with chrome accents around the front of the cab and on the lower portions of the cab doors. The tandem rear-axle job was equipped with a 1500-gpm pump and 2500-gallon water tank. *Scott Mattson photo*

Grumman was known more for its pumpers and Aerialcats, but it did construct at least two heavy rescue apparatus. This "walk-around" rescue was built for Lovettsville, Virginia, on a 1991 International 4900 two-door chassis. The lime rig was part of a package deal that included a Panther II pumper. *Mike Sanders photo*

This walk-around rescue on a 1992 International 4900 four-door chassis was built for Marmora, New Jersey. This faithful customer purchased several pieces of apparatus from Grumman, including Ford C-Series pumpers and a Panther II pumper-tanker. *Scott Mattson photo*

Cinnaminson, New Jersey, received this unique apparatus in 1991. The low profile unit was built on a Simon-Duplex D-450-T chassis. It was equipped with a 1500-gpm pump and 250-gallon water tank. The 85-foot articulating Snorkel was nestled into a well-stocked body, which featured ground ladders stored flat and on the beam. Note the pre-piped deluge gun mounted over the pump panel. Cinnaminson also operated a Grumman pumper on a 1988 Duplex D-500 Vanguard chassis. *Scott Mattson photo*

The Greenfield Fire Company in Bern Township, Pennsylvania, received this standard four-door Panther II with raised roof in 1991. Painted white over teal, the apparatus was equipped with a 1500-gpm pump and 1000-gallon water tank. Crosslays were mounted at an ergonomic height over the top of a transverse compartment. A Mars 888 light was recessed into the front grille of the cab. *Rick Rudisill photo*

The state of Kentucky was a solid sales territory for Howe, Oren, and then Grumman. Although the majority of rigs were commercial jobs, many custom apparatus were delivered as well. Union received this compact four-door Panther II in 1991. Serial number 18553 featured a 1250-gpm pump with top-mount controls and carried 1000 gallons of water. *Kent Parrish photo*

Kelowna in British Columbia, Canada, received this 102-foot Aerialcat in 1991. Built on a Panther I chassis, serial number 18631 was equipped with a 1250-gpm pump and 250-gallon water tank. HME was now the primary chassis supplier and cab finisher for the Aerialcats. The automatic outrigger leveling system utilized by the Aerialcats was similar in design to the one used by Grumman Aeronautical Engineering on the Lunar Landing Module that landed on the moon in 1969. Swiveling footpads provided balance on uneven terrain. Rotation short-jack and interlock safety systems were optional. *Shane MacKichan photo*

The Ashburn Volunteer Fire Department in Loudon County, Virginia, is very well equipped. The photographer took this shot of his department's 1991 Panther II Firecat pumper. Engine 6 featured a long four-door cab. The white over yellow unit was equipped with a 1250-gpm pump and 600-gallon water tank. It carried serial number 18579. Because of an aggressive replacement program, the rig was placed out of service in 2004. Grumman often stamped various model numbers on the builder's plate inside the cab. For example, an "F-12" was a 1250-gpm Firecat or an "FC-1500" designated a 1500-gpm Firecat. *Mike Sanders photo*

Baltimore County, Maryland, has operated numerous Grumman pumpers throughout the years. Six pumpers were delivered between 1978 and 1982 on Pemfab and Duplex chassis with four-door cabs. Five of those were equipped with 50-foot Readi-Tower devices. Pictured is a 1980 model on a Duplex D-300 chassis with 1250-gpm pump, 500-gallon water tank, and 50-foot Readi-Tower. *Frank Wegloski photo*

Baltimore County would later receive a total of five Grumman Panther II pumpers with standard four-door cabs and change its color scheme from white over yellow to white over red. This 1991 model carried 750 gallons of water on an extended wheelbase. Some late-model Panther tilt-cabs could be found with rectangular side air vents to allow for more efficient engine cooling. Many others had them added after the fact. *Howard Meile photo*

Grumman also produced the industry standard 100-foot straight stick aerial by simply extending each ladder section of the 95-foot model. The city of Hamilton in Ontario, Canada, received this 100-foot Aerialcat in 1991. Painted chrome yellow, it was built on a Spartan Gladiator chassis. Hamilton required that its new apparatus be subjected to the stringent testing performed by the Underwriters Laboratory of Canada. Grumman agreed to the testing and this unit became the first American built ladder to pass Canadian review. At least one other 100-foot model was produced. *Dave Stewardson photo*

Allouez, Wisconsin, received this pumper with standard four-door Panther II cab in 1991. It was equipped with a 1500-gpm pump and 500-gallon water tank. The apparatus was painted white with an orange cab roof and striping. The top-mount control panel had black vinyl facing and a hydraulic rack on the officer's side stored ground ladders up and out of the way. Although on custom Grumman chassis, Panther II pumpers were sometimes designated as Firecats as well. *Paul Barrett photo*

Grumman also made pumper deliveries in Canada. Dundas, Ontario, received this standard four-door Panther II in 1992. It was equipped with a 1050-gpm pump and 500-gallon water tank. Grumman advertised the Firecat 1900 as a custom pumper that met or exceeded the new NFPA 1901 standards for fire apparatus. By following a basic option list, it was available for $148,000. It is roughly estimated that Grumman delivered no more than 200 total Panther II pumpers. *Dave Stewardson photo*

This monstrous pumper-tanker was one of the largest such apparatus built by Grumman. The 1991 Firecat was delivered to the Odessa Fire Company in Delaware. It was built on a Simon-Duplex D-500-T Vanguard chassis and featured a big 1750-gpm pump with 3000-gallon water tank. This rig was almost self sufficient on the fireground. In the following year, Odessa would add a Panther II pumper to its impressive fleet. *Scott Mattson photo*

It is no surprise that Roanoke City was a loyal Grumman customer. The department took delivery of six new units in 1991, including five of these Panther II pumpers with standard four-door cabs. Serial numbers 18681 through 18685 were equipped with 1500-gpm pumps and 500-gallon water tanks. Previous Roanoke pumper deliveries were built on a mix of Duplex, Hendrickson, and Spartan chassis. *Mike Sanders photo*

Roanoke City also assigned this 121-foot Aerialcat straight stick to Ladder 7 in 1991. Serial number 18476 was built on a Panther I chassis and did not feature a pump or tank. Grumman only built approximately 15 total straight stick aerials. The heavy-duty design was just too expensive to compete in the traditional ladder market. *Steve Hagy photo*

Three short wheelbased Panther II pumpers with standard four-door cabs were delivered to the United States Army post at Fort Ritchie, Maryland, in 1991. They were equipped with 1000-gpm pumps, 350-gallon water tanks, and 30-gallon foam cells. The lime units were assigned serial numbers 18466 through 18468. Fort Ritchie, whose primary responsibilities were information systems and training, was closed as an active Army installation in 1998. The present locations of these rigs are unknown. *Howard Meile photo*

The Ringing Hill Fire Company of Lower Pottsgrove Township, Pennsylvania, took delivery of this 102-foot Aerialcat in 1991. Serial number 18478 was built on a Panther I chassis. It was equipped with a 1500-gpm pump and 250-gallon water tank. The Aerialcat three-section ladder tower featured 80,000-psi tensile strength steel construction with a built-in allowance for 50-mile-per-hour winds and a 1/2-inch ice buildup on the entire structure. The platform itself had a pivot mount centered below the basket to reduce structural tension, reduce basket droop, and provide greater stability. *Rick Rudisill photo*

The Ford C-Series had been a popular choice of chassis for many fire apparatus manufacturers and customers alike for over 30 years, but its great run had come to an end. Manchester, Ohio, received this canopy-cab Firecat in 1991. The 1250-gpm pumper had a top-mount control panel with black vinyl facing. The apparatus carried 1000 gallons of water. Sporting a two-tone white and red paint scheme, Unit 4 was assigned serial number 18572. *Steve Hagy photo*

With the demise of the Ford C-Series, the International commercial chassis would become a staple in small town firehouses across America. New NFPA standards eliminated riding the tailboard and required all firefighters to be seated and belted on existing apparatus. All new apparatus were to have fully enclosed cabs. Salem, Indiana, took delivery of this four-door International 4900 in 1992. Assigned serial number 18739, the Firecat was equipped with a 1250-gpm pump and 1000-gallon water tank. *Kent Parrish photo*

The Lake Dreamland Fire District in Louisville, Kentucky, received this delivery in 1992. The apparatus was built on a Panther I chassis. It was equipped with a 1500-gpm pump and 500-gallon water tank. An uncommon option in modern fire apparatus design was the dual booster reel configuration. The 54-foot articulating Squrt was a popular device among Louisville area departments. It provided for a versatile first-out piece of apparatus. This unit carried serial number 18714. *Kent Parrish photo*

The Millstone Valley Fire Company in New Jersey received this Panther II Triple Threat pumper in 1992. Serial number 18525 had a long four-door cab with raised roof. The 1500-gpm rear-mount pumper carried 1000 gallons of water and 60 gallons of foam. The rear pump panel and booster reel compartment were protected by roll-up doors. The Grumman Triple Threat pumper had a modular body available in galvanized steel or aluminum construction with over 142 cubic feet of compartment space and hose bed capacity for up to 3000 feet of hose. *Scott Mattson photo*

This 92-foot mid-mount Aerialcat was delivered to Shrewsbury, New Jersey, in 1992 on a Spartan Gladiator chassis. It was equipped with a 1500-gpm rear-mount pump and 150-gallon water tank. The apparatus was assigned serial number 18687. The mid-mount platforms were rated at 1000 pounds. Ground ladders were stored on the sides of the apparatus to decrease the traveling height of the apparatus. Grumman built less than 10 mid-mount Aerialcats. *Scott Mattson photo*

This Panther II pumper with standard four-door cab was delivered to the small town of Aurora, Indiana, in 1992. The 1500-gpm pumper had top-mount controls and carried 1000 gallons. Engine 516 was assigned serial number 18782. A portable monitor stand was carried on the front bumper extension and the popular "Taz" cartoon character adorned the crew doors. *Kent Parrish photo*

Lancaster, Kentucky, received this Panther II rescue-pumper with long four-door cab in May of 1992. The apparatus was equipped with a 1500-gpm pump and 500-gallon water tank. The body featured full depth and height compartments with a flat back design. Serial number 18763 also carried a two-bottle cascade system and 12,000-pound winch in the front bumper extension. *Kent Parrish photo*

This Firecat rescue-pumper was delivered to Cold Spring, Kentucky, in 1992. The department has since merged with a neighboring fire district and is now known as Central Campbell. It was built on a Simon-Duplex D-350 chassis. Serial number 18779 was equipped with a 1500-gpm pump, 700-gallon water tank, and 50-gallon foam cell. The body had full depth and height rescue-style compartments with a flat back design and special high sides, a trend still a few years ahead of its time. *Kent Parrish photo*

The town of Greensburg, Indiana, received this 102-foot Aerialcat in 1992. It had a Panther I cab on a Simon-Duplex chassis, which was still utilized occasionally if pricing was an issue. Serial number 18639 was equipped with a 1500-gpm pump and 200-gallon water tank. Grumman built over 200 total Aerialcats. International deliveries included units for Africa, Mexico, and Saudi Arabia. When Grumman closed its doors, KME Fire Apparatus purchased the major assets and offered to pick up the warranties on the Aerialcats in exchange for the design and rights to the name. To this day the KME Aerialcat is produced at the Roanoke facility. *Kent Parrish photo*

Grumman stopped taking new fire apparatus orders after closing of the Emergency Products division was announced in December of 1991. The Roanoke plant shut its doors in September of 1992 once a backlog of nearly 150 units was completed. Unfortunately, the Grumman files did not survive and many departments claim to have the "last Grumman off the line." However, with a serial number of 18794, this standard four-door Panther II pumper for Clifton Forge, Virginia, is believed to possibly be the last order completed by Grumman. The 1500-gpm rig carried 750 gallons of water. It must be noted that KME did complete a handful of "Frankenstein" pumpers in Pennsylvania utilizing Grumman remnants. While they had definitive Grumman characteristics, they were listed as 1993 models and carried KME markings. The Grumman "look" is still evident in many of the successful fire apparatus manufacturers of today. *Kent Parrish photo*

More Great Titles From

Iconografix

All Iconografix books are available from direct mail specialty book dealers and bookstores worldwide, or can be ordered from the publisher. For book trade and distribution information or to add your name to our mailing list and receive a **FREE CATALOG** contact:

Iconografix, Inc.
PO Box 446, Dept BK
Hudson, WI, 54016

Telephone: (715) 381-9755,
(800) 289-3504 (USA),
Fax: (715) 381-9756
info@iconografixinc.com
www.iconografixinc.com

More great books from Iconografix

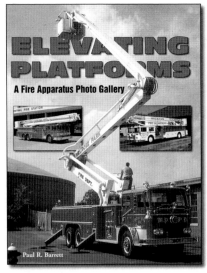

ELEVATING PLATFORMS
A Fire Apparatus Photo Gallery

Paul R. Barrett

ISBN 1-58388-164-6

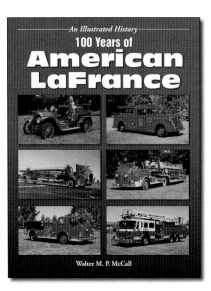

An Illustrated History
100 Years of American LaFrance

Walter M. P. McCall

ISBN 1-58388-139-5

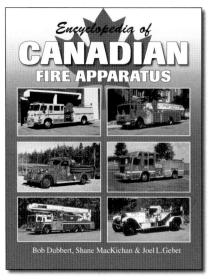

Encyclopedia of
CANADIAN FIRE APPARATUS

Bob Dubbert, Shane MacKichan & Joel L. Gebet

ISBN 1-58388-119-0

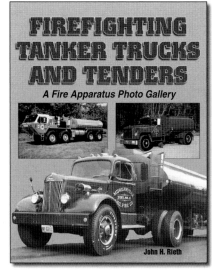

FIREFIGHTING TANKER TRUCKS AND TENDERS
A Fire Apparatus Photo Gallery

John H. Rieth

ISBN 1-58388-138-7

Iconografix, Inc.
P.O. Box 446, Dept BK,
Hudson, WI 54016
For a free catalog call:
1-800-289-3504
info@iconografixinc.com
www.iconografixinc.com

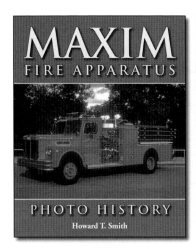

MAXIM FIRE APPARATUS
PHOTO HISTORY

Howard T. Smith

ISBN 1-58388-111-5

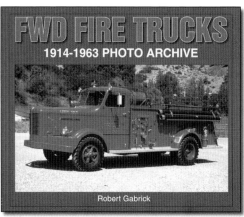

FWD FIRE TRUCKS
1914-1963 PHOTO ARCHIVE

Robert Gabrick

ISBN 1-58388-156-5

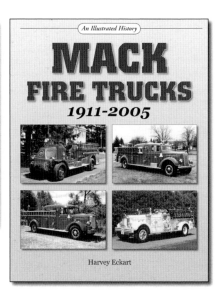

An Illustrated History
MACK FIRE TRUCKS
1911-2005

Harvey Eckart

ISBN 1-58388-157-3